For cooks and poets everywhere

Atheneum Books for Young Readers
An imprint of Simon & Schuster Children's Publishing Division
1230 Avenue of the Americas
New York, New York 10020

Book design by Ann Bobco

The text of this book is set in Deepdene.
The illustrations are rendered in watercolor.

Printed in Hong Kong
2 4 6 8 10 9 7 5 3 1

Library of Congress Cataloging-in-Publication Data
Mathers, Petra.
A cake for Herbie / by Petra Mathers.—1st ed.
p. cm.
"An Anne Schwartz book."
Summary: With the encouragement of his friend, Herbie spends days
writing poems about food for a contest, and although he does not win,
he does find an appreciative audience.
ISBN 0-689-83017-3
[1. Ducks—Fiction. 2. Animals—Fiction. 3. Poetry—Fiction.
4. Contests—Fiction.] I. Title. PZ7.M42475Cak 2000 [E]—dc21 99-24881

FIRST
EDITION

A Cake for Herbie

by petra mathers

An Anne Schwartz Book
ATHENEUM BOOKS FOR YOUNG READERS

Once a week Lottie and her best friend Herbie drove across
Moose Bay Bridge to shop for groceries in town.

At Hawkie's Market, Herbie saw a poster.

"I'd like to win that cake," he said.
"Can you write a poem?" asked Lottie.
"I think so," said Herbie.

"You know how I always make up things
like: Listen to those cookies shout,
Open up, let us out!"

"I thought I heard something," said Lottie.

"C for cookies, that's it!" cried Herbie. "I'll write poems about food, one for each letter of the alphabet."

Only three days until the contest!
Herbie worked hard.
Thinking made his head hot.

The cold made him hungry.

After a big bowl of chocolate pudding, Herbie wrote till dawn.

"Lottie, listen, I got all the way to K:
You don't need mustard
for karamel kustard."

"I like it," said Lottie, "but caramel
custard starts with C."
"Oh," said Herbie. "I knew that."

The night before the contest,
Herbie had terrible dreams.

I'm so glad Lottie will be there,
he thought, turning over.

But that night Lottie got sick.

"How can I do it without you?"
 asked Herbie.
"Think of the cake and take a deep breath,"
 whispered Lottie.

"Gummy Bear, Honey Pie, Ice Cream, Jell-O. Oh, oh, oh, my knees feel like Jell-O," groaned Herbie.

"Name?" someone asked.
"Herbie."
"You're late, here is your tag. Find your seat quietly, please."

". . . now I know no one but one gnome,
no one knows I know this gnome,
only the gnome knows that I know him."
Wow! thought Herbie.

When it was Herbie's turn,
he took a deep breath.
"From Herbie's Kitchen
A to Z," he said.

"A: Artie chews,
Artie swallows,
Artichokes."

"B: Inside me lives
the Belly Beast.
It growls five times
a day at least."

"C: When you hear the cookies shout . . ."
"All the way to Z?" someone whispered.
"Belly beast, shouting cookies, who is this duck?"
"How about E for END?" someone else said a little louder.

"K is for kruel," Herbie said, and left.

He didn't care where he was going.
All he wanted was a place to hide.

After a while Herbie heard a voice.
"Holy mackerel, you scared me.
You must be freezing . . .

. . . bet you're hungry, too.
Well, you've come to the right place."

"Hey, look, you guys, this is Herbie.
I found him sitting on the curbie," shouted his new friend.

"Hello, Herbie, I'm sweaty Betty.
You look like you need some spaghetti."

Herbie felt better right away.
He sat down and looked around.

"Ten more minutes on the griddle.
  It's still too soggy in the middle."

"Oh, I'm grumpy!
  Why is this caramel custard so lumpy?"

Herbie jumped up.
"At least there's no mustard
in your caramel custard," he said.

"Did you hear that, Gus?"
"You bet I did, he's one of us!"

When the Ship's Inn closed, everyone sat down to dinner.
"Tell us another, Herbie," they said.
And Herbie did, all the way from A to Z.

"Bravo, Herbie!" everyone shouted, and
a big cake appeared.
"Just look at that," said Herbie.
"I can't wait to tell . . .

Herbie barely took time to thank his
friends. He had only one thought—
to get back to Lottie.

The road seemed endless.
The cake sat next to him, still warm
and smelling delicious.

"Lottie, you're up!" cried Herbie,
jumping out of the car.
"How are you?"

"I'm much better, dear," Lottie said.
"But what about you? You look like you won
and ate the cake. Come in quick, I can't wait
to hear all about it."